CHIPMUNKS
KW-181

Title page: *Chipmunks are quickly becoming popular pets around the world—and for good reason! Chipmunks are lively and interesting, cute and captivating rodents which breed well and have hearty dispositions.*

Photo credits: *All photos by Michael Gilroy except as follows: Burkhard Kahl (contents page and pp. 40,49); Christine Wright, Latchington NR Chelmsford, Essex (pp. 27, 71).*

Artwork by: *Richard Davis and John R. Quinn.*

Distributed in the UNITED STATES by T.F.H. Publications, Inc., One T.F.H. Plaza, Neptune City, NJ 07753; in CANADA to the Pet Trade by H & L Pet Supplies Inc., 27 Kingston Crescent, Kitchener, Ontario N2B 2T6; Rolf C. Hagen Ltd., 3225 Sartelon Street, Montreal 382 Quebec; in CANADA to the Book Trade by Macmillan of Canada (A Division of Canada Publishing Corporation), 164 Commander Boulevard, Agincourt, Ontario M1S 3C7; in ENGLAND by T.F.H. Publications Limited, Cliveden House/Priors Way/Bray, Maidenhead, Berkshire SL6 2HP, England; in AUSTRALIA AND THE SOUTH PACIFIC by T.F.H. (Australia) Pty. Ltd., Box 149, Brookvale 2100 N.S.W., Australia; in NEW ZEALAND by Ross Haines & Son, Ltd., 18 Monmouth Street, Grey Lynn, Auckland 2, New Zealand; in the PHILIPPINES by Bio-Research, 5 Lippay Street, San Lorenzo Village, Makati Rizal; in SOUTH AFRICA by Multipet Pty. Ltd., 30 Turners Avenue, Durban 4001. Published by T.F.H. Publications, Inc. Manufactured in the United States of America by T.F.H. Publications, Inc.

CHIPMUNKS

By Chris Henwood

Chipmunks are by far one of the more adorable rodents available to the pet owner of today; as such, they are welcomed into almost any home and taken to with affection by many.

Contents

GENERAL INTRODUCTION

Chipmunks are one of the many members of the group of mammals known as rodents. As a whole rodents are a highly adaptable group of creatures, and to understand the chipmunk totally, I think it is important that you understand what a rodent is and how it is different from other mammals. I also hope that this introduction will help you to understand why your pet chipmunk does certain strange things.

A feature common to ALL rodents is their ability to gnaw. In fact, the word rodent itself is derived from the Latin word *rodere*, which means "to gnaw." A rodent's ability to gnaw is made possible by the unusual arrangement of the teeth. The sharp incisor teeth at the front of the mouth are responsible for rodents' capacity to chew through just about anything. The molar teeth at the back of the mouth, or the pre-molars if these are present (not all rodents have pre-molars), grind the food into

smaller pieces for swallowing. Between the molars and the incisors there is a gap, known as the diostema, where there are no teeth at all. This gap allows the cheeks to be closed in behind the incisors, thus enabling the rodents to continue gnawing while only selective items are being swallowed or placed into the cheek pouches, as in the case of chipmunks and hamsters.

Since the incisors are in constant and very heavy use, they gradually become worn down. To compensate for this, they continue growing throughout the animal's life. For this reason, it is vitally important that the upper and lower incisor teeth actually meet at the front of the mouth. Should, for any reason whatsoever the teeth be misaligned, the animal will no longer be able to eat and

Facing Page: A proper diet, with plenty of nuts included, helps to keep the chipmunk's ever-growing front incisors at a safe and comfortable length.

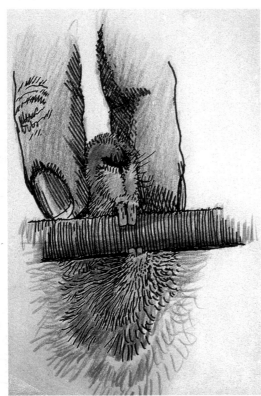

As with chinchillas, gerbils, and other rodents, a chipmunk's teeth must be filed to a proper length (by an experienced professional) if they should grow too long. The best prevention is to give your chipmunk plenty of safe, recommended objects to chew.

the distorted teeth will strike the opposite jaw. If this is not noticed and dealt with, you will often find that the teeth have continued growing and have actually grown into the jaw, causing great discomfort and eventually, because the animal cannot eat properly, death.

In common with other plant-eating animals, rodents feeding on various plant material are actually incapable of digesting the carbohydrate present in the form of cellulose. Although rodents lack the elaborate stomach systems of many of these plant-eaters, they still rely on a beneficial group of bacteria to undertake this task. These bacteria possess the enzymes known as cellulases that break down the cellulose. They are located in the caecal sacs of the large intestine (this vaguely corresponds to the appendix of the human). Because in some rodents vitamin B_{12} is not directly available to the animals but has to be synthesized by bacteria in the colon, some actually re-ingest the partially digested food after it has been voided from the body via the anus. These droppings are relatively loose and contain not only partly digested food but also vitamins synthesized by the bacteria. They are quite unlike the dry "normal" droppings associated with rodents. As the owner of a chipmunk, it is important to realize that consumption of faecal material, a practice that is actually known as coprophagy, is essential to the health of your animal.

Chipmunks enjoy a large variety of fruits, vegetables, and nuts. For best nutrition it has been found that feeding moderate amounts of many foods is best, with variety being important.

Chipmunks are ground or terrestrial animals, but they also forage in trees; in this sense they can be considered to be intermediate between the tree squirrels, such as the Grey and Red, and true ground dwelling squirrels as, for example, the prairie dog.

All chipmunks have large internal cheek pouches, black and white facial stripes and a varying number of stripes on the back and sides of their small bodies. Chipmunks are found in North America, with the single exception of one species (although several subspecies) that is widespread in Eurasia. It is this latter species, commonly known as the Siberian Chipmunk that the major portion of this book will be about.

At one time chipmunks were placed into two genera: *Eutamias* for the chipmunks of Western North America and Eurasia and *Tamias* for those of Eastern North America. Most authorities still retain both of these. However, recent evidence indicates that all chipmunks are so closely related as to make their separation into these two different groups

At first glance, the chipmunk's most conspicuous characteristic is its striped back and head.

The trend today is to house pets in an environment that resembles their natural habitat in both looks and conditions. Your local pet store has safe, non-toxic climbing branches, bedding, and other accessories to help you safely achieve a successful simulation.

unwarranted. I don't really think that this matters to us, the pet keepers of this wonderful group of rodents, but it may explain things you may read in other books.

One would be hard-pressed to find a more appropriate pet for a youngster than a hand-reared baby chipmunk.

The actual name "chipmunk" is of uncertain origin, while it usually is attributed to the "chip" call note of members of the genus; more plausibly it was derived from an American Native Indian word *"achiitaman"* or

"chetaman", which, I am told, means head first, in reference to the way in which the chipmunk and other squirrels descend tree trunks.

To my mind, chipmunks make lively, colourful companions and are relatively new to the pet world and for this reason they are still rather expensive when compared to other small rodents. However, they are now being bred much more easily in captivity and with the appearance of colour mutations, it is likely that both availability and thus price will change for the better. Adult individuals can prove difficult animals to handle but stock obtained young often become embarrassingly tame and down right nosey. They have endless agility, making them very entertaining and pleasant to live with. I think that I should give one word of warning here. Once you own a chipmunk, you may never wish to be without one again and some people

If obtained at an early age, a chipmunk will take very well to its human protector; and view him as its close and trusted friend.

I know are very sad at having to part with any of the babies they have bred. But there does come a point when some have to go.

As I have said, the major part of this book is about the Siberian Chipmunk—*Eutamias sibiricus,* mainly because this is the most readily obtainable species. However, almost all the different species and subspecies mentioned in the book can be treated in basically the same way. The most common of the subspecies available in the United Kingdom is that of the Korean and should you be offered an animal as a Korean Chipmunk and be told that this is different from the Siberian, please remember my words: the Korean and the Siberian are the same.

As a general rule, the Siberian Chipmunk's fur is short and soft to the touch. It is light brown to reddish-gold in colour and is distinguished by its five black stripes, alternating with two brown and two white. It measures 14-19 cms in length with a bushy tail of approximately the same length. Adults weigh about 100-125 grams.

There are a number of subspecies of the Siberian Chipmunk from various parts of the Far East. The species as a whole is described as occurring from the Bering Sea to the central Asian deserts and including Manchuria, Korea, Shantung, central China and on the islands of Sakhalin, Iturup and Hokkaido.

The official scientific description of the species as a whole reflects this very wide distribution and the fact that many different colour variations occur. The following is a combination of different descriptions and observations that I have observed in the British Museum of Natural History. I hope that it will help you to understand how complex is the question of where in the wild a particular animal may come from.

Colour Top of the head varies from greyish buff chestnut to a more intense rust-brown with buff mottling in the various subspecies.

Eye surrounded by a white to whitish ring. A whitish stripe with a buff tone at the margins from the ring to the nose. Another stripe runs from the posterior ventral corner of the ring to the base of the ear. A chestnut-black-brown stripe runs from the posterior margin of the ring to the ear, ending in the middle of the inner side of the ear. A dark-chestnut stripe is bordered by more chestnut of varying intensity from the anterior part of the muzzle, beneath the ring around the eye, and widens posteriorly. Lower parts of the cheeks are a dirty buffish white. Posterior parts of the cheeks are sometimes more yellow-rust coloured. Occiput behind the ears ash grey with a rust tinge. Five chestnut-black longitudinal stripes run from the occiput to the middle of the back. Middle stripe from occiput to the base of the tail. The stripes next to the middle stripe begin on the shoulders and continue to the posterior

Although there are many species of chipmunks, these various groups are so closely related as to make the distinction unimportant for the pet owner. Here is an artist's rendition of the Siberian Chipmunk, which according to the author is the same as the Korean Chipmunk.

part of the middle of the back. The lateral stripes begin anterior to the base of the forelegs and continue to the sides of the buttocks. Between the five dark stripes there are four lighter stripes, the anterior part of the light stripes being whitish buff and the posterior part more reddish rust coloured. The intensity of the rust shade varies in different subspecies between cinnamon buff and cinnamon, sayal brown and orange cinnamon. The whole posterior part of the back and the haunches are reddish rust of varying intensity. Yellowish rust tones are also present on the flanks. This colour is sharply defined from the dirty whitish tone on the belly. The tail is a chestnut grey, with the tips of the hairs white. The roots of these hairs are usually a pale buff rust followed by a broad black band and then white tip. There are also many completely black hairs with whitish tips. There are also rust buff hairs especially on the

Always keep in mind that your pet chipmunk is still by nature attuned to its "wild" instincts; proper care will mean taking these into consideration.

ventral side while the dorsal side of the feet are grey chestnut buff and the claws are greyish rust. Whiskers are grey or black.

So that's it. As a general guide I have found that the chipmunks of the west and the island populations appear to be more sandy or cinnamon and also finer boned than those of the Northeast and Korea. Naturally, others may disagree.

To understand the behaviour of our pet chipmunks, I think that it is important to look at part of the behaviour of the species in the wild. In this way we can more easily see why certain requirements should be provided and how we can improve their lives—in other words make their homes with us as near to the wild as possible.

In the wild, the Siberian is a diurnal animal. The daily life appears to differ from season to season and according to the weather of the day. In the spring they come out of their burrow

In addition to making their homes as natural as possible, it is important to keep their diet that way also. To make your pet-keeping hobby even more enjoyable and rewarding, learn as much as you can about the chipmunk's natural habits and adopt them into its care.

only when the sun has had a chance to warm up the ground a little. The main period of activity is from approximately 10 in the morning to 4 in the afternoon. By sunset they are all back in their burrows. They also remain in them when the weather is wet or very windy.

In summer they are up and about before daybreak, in fact just as soon as it

Chipmunks are known as ground squirrels; however, they do have a good climbing ability. All chipmunk housing should have a climbing branch included.

becomes light enough to see. They are very active—jumping, washing and chasing about in addition to the normal feeding and mating behaviour. Between 12 and 2 they appear to return to their burrows for a midday sleep re-appearing again at about 2 and remaining active and feeding until sunset when they return to their burrows for the night.

In summer and autumn, they appear to be less concerned by the rain and wind than during the spring. This may be that the areas in which this species has been most closely observed in the wild have quite a high rainfall during these months but rainfall that is not particularly cold and therefore not too unpleasant. During the autumn, it appears that their behaviour patterns are similar to those of the summer, making the most of the warm daylight hours to feed and collect/store food for the oncoming winter.

Winter behaviour really does appear to depend on where the animals are. In some areas of Siberia they hibernate totally from October through to February, while in many areas they are up and out of their burrows feeding whenever the weather is dry and mild, remaining the rest of their time in the burrows. These burrows appear not to be very complex systems. The entrances are usually at the base of tree stumps. The burrow descends at an angle of approximately 45° immediately after the entrance. It then continues almost horizontally and ends in a rounded chamber which contains the nest area. Side galleries appear to be rare and there are never more than three. The burrows usually have one exit. The galleries are some 60-400 cms long, and the chamber about 20-40 cms wide and 40-100 cms underground. Some burrows have small corridors filled with excrement. Food reserves are kept in chambers, very rarely in the galleries. The nest is usually an open chamber with the bedding material in the centre.

The entrance to the burrows is usually hidden by some form of vegetation.

Newborn chipmunks are very vulnerable. In the wild they would be well-hidden within the chipmunk's burrows. In your home it is important to provide a nest box for breeding.

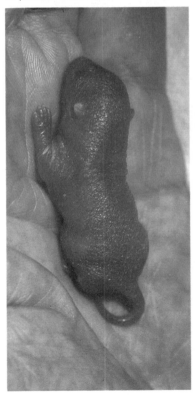

HOUSING

In the wild, chipmunks prefer to live in underground tunnels and burrows with a nesting chamber or in hollow tree stumps. They line their nests with soft foliage for warmth and comfort. Generally each

This is one of the author's indoor cages. Note the good height and abundance of climbing branches and barks.

pair has their own nesting area. They do appear, at least in some species, to live in fairly close association with other pairs or families.

In captivity, chipmunks are best housed outside in large, high, wooden and wire cages rather along the lines of bird aviaries. But this is not the only way in which to retain the chipmunk and there are very many people who keep them in much smaller areas than this. I certainly would not like to state that this is the only way in which to keep them and thus prevent someone who lives in a flat or apartment from owning some of these wonderful creatures. For this reason I shall give you as many different ways of keeping chipmunks as I have been told about. Any measurements you see in the text are regarded as a guideline and a minimum size that I would give to my own animals. The first rule of caging chipmunks is: the bigger the cage, the better.

All-wire cages are ideal for chipmunks. Discretion must be exercised when determining the proper width of the bars; aim for bars no further than 1 cm. apart.

All Wire Indoor Cage

This type of cage is limited only by the size that you can either buy or make and more important, bearing in mind what I said above, the amount of space that you have. I would suggest that the minimum size that you should consider be 60 cms high by 20 cms square. Very few commercial cages made in this size are designed for chipmunks; however, a number are made and sold in the pet shops for Cockatiels, Lovebirds, etc., and by hunting around and adapting them slightly, these make ideal chipmunk cages. The most important item to look out for is the width of the bars. I would suggest that you aim for a cage with bars no further than 1 cm apart.

You may of course decide to make a cage of your own. I have found that the easiest way to do this is to make it out of a wire known as Twilweld or Weldmesh. This is a strong squared mesh that is so strong it is able to support itself, thus not requiring any wooden or metal framing. It may be fastened together

easily by using pliers and special clips known as 'C' clips. I would suggest a cage at least as tall as it is wide. However, again the size can depend on the area in which you wish it to be sited. One side of the cage should have a hole cut in it and a piece of mesh at least 10 cms larger than the gap placed over it as a door; again this can be fastened to the cage by using 'C' clips along one edge, thus creating a hinge. A fastening may be easily made using a wire frame sold in most department stores for hanging small plates on the wall. A series of simple shelves may be

Here we see the firm-footed ease with which a chipmunk can perch upon a climbing branch to get a better view.

placed inside at various heights either using wood or by stretching more mesh between three of the walls, and twigs and branches can be provided for climbing. The cage will have an all wire bottom and this may be elevated a few centimeters on wood to enable droppings and urine to fall on to newspaper or sawdust on the tray below.

A nest box should be provided for each animal to be housed and these may be hung on the inside or outside of the cage with a suitable hole cut in the wire to allow access for the animal.

Nest boxes themselves may either be made or purchased. However, I have yet to come across any nest boxes actually sold for chipmunks. I would

Wooden Indoor Cages

To my mind these are second best to the above but this is only my opinion. The best sized cage would again be as large as possible. However, I have seen some very suitable cages manufactured for one or two chipmunks. The best

Nest boxes are essential to any chipmunk cage; they provide a place for pairs to breed and a source of confidence and protection for singles and pairs alike.

therefore suggest that you hunt around for Cockatiel or Lovebird nest boxes made of wood. Both of these have proved suitable for my own animals.

of these was 120 cms × 60 cms × 60 cms. This cage had only one side made of wire, the rest being of wood and also had a built-in but exterior nest box. The roof

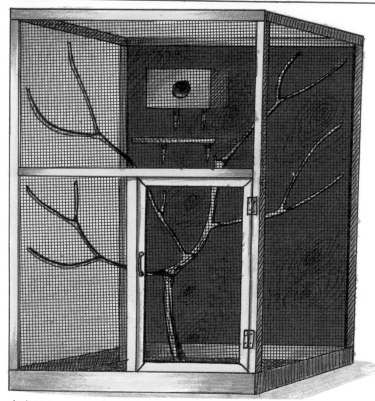

Indoor cages can be made or purchased in a variety of shapes and sizes. This one is as high as it is wide, an excellent feature at a six-foot width. It also has a wooden nesting box set high with a shelf for easy access and a door set low for easy cleaning; it is a well-planned construction.

was removable and therefore the owner was able to remove it for cleaning and the introduction of new branches and twigs— always a problem once the chipmunks have begun to chew them.

Outdoor Sheds or Aviaries

There are several different ways of arranging the outdoor accommodation for chipmunks. A large outdoor area attached to a shed with a small indoor

Outdoor aviaries offer the pet owner a wide variety of selection. They are limited only by the size of the property on which they are placed and the creative ability of the builder. Function should precede all, however, so keep in mind the points mentioned in this text.

area, or vice versa. A total outdoor area in a sheltered spot with no attached shed but very well built frostproof nest boxes. These can be all-purpose built or adapted from a bird aviary. All of these may be of different sizes to suit your own situation.

Aviaries may be very simple or very complex depending on the ability of the builder or what you can afford to buy. I would suggest that you try to have one that is pleasing to look at both to yourself and others. Nothing is worse than the enclosure in which you retain your beloved animals being so ugly that people don't remember the animals after their visit—just "that awful shed".

My own personal favourite is either a rectangular or hexagonal outdoor area with a small shed attached. The outside area should have a paved or wired floor to prevent either the chipmunks burrowing out or wild

Your outdoor pen is best set up in a sheltered area, such as against the weather-protected side of a wall, with a roof that slopes downward from it.

This very attractive shelter was well planned with a foundation of brick to keep out pests and predators. (Owned by Mrs. Christine Wright, Latchingdon NR Chelmsford, Essex.)

rodents and other vermin burrowing in. I then like to see a double row of bricks around the entire area on which the wire framework stands. The height should ideally be for you rather than for the chipmunks; after all, you will be entering the shed and running to see and be with the animals.

There is nothing more uncomfortable than standing for a period with your back bent. Therefore if you are 6' I would suggest a height of 6'4" for the roof.

Any access door should be covered by an entrance porch; however, should your garden be small then this may be better resolved by having the entrance to the run via the shed. Thus you may be able to have a separate area in the shed for this.

I would suggest a shed of say 6′ square and an outside enclosure of at least 4′ square. Ideally I say to people 12′ × 6′ or 12′ × 4′ but in these days of increasingly small gardens this is not always a suitable size. The shed should be mounted on a paved or similar floor. The shed roof north facing wall should be covered by stout plastic on the outside to protect the inhabitants, and you, when you are feeding them, from the worst of the weather. There should be two entrances from the shed to the outside area—one at ground level and one at about your own shoulder

should slope AWAY from the enclosure and should be of wood with a felt or weatherproof covering; never use metal for the roof as this is both too hot and too noisy for chipmunks. Approximately ¼-½ of the outside area roof and all the

Facing Page and Above: Whether kept in an indoor wire cage or an outdoor natural setting, chipmunks are easily contented, easy-to-keep, fun and rewarding animals.

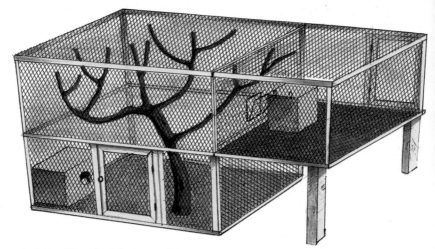

A cage with an introduction chamber and a trap door makes breeding easier. Such a structure allows for safe acclimation and introduction of the female to the male and an uninfluenced placement of the male into the receptive female's cage by simply opening the trap door.

height. The latter should be within easy reach of branches in the outside run.

The outside run should have a floor well covered with a deep litter of peat and/or bark chippings in which the chipmunks can dig and bury their food. It should be furnished with a good amount—basically as much as you can get in—of branches, twigs, hollow logs, etc. These should be washed before being included in the run and should be of a type of wood such as apple or pear or another fruit. The leaves may be left on as this will add to the interest of it for the chipmunks. One nest box per individual should be positioned along one wall of the outside aviary. I suggest that they be at about your own shoulder height. This will allow you to inspect them with ease. They should also be all at the same height as this will prevent fighting over possession of the highest one. I recommend that they also be at least two chipmunk body lengths apart, for the same reason.

The interior of the shed should be divided into two or possibly three different areas. The part nearest the outside run should be wired off to allow a floor-to-roof indoor cage. This will give the chipmunks an area in which to exercise during bad weather with nestboxes available to each of the individual runs allowing free movement from both in and outside. The rear and the major portion of the shed can be used either for storage area and food preparation or divided yet again to give a smaller indoor run that may be used for individuals that for any reason have to be separated from the main population. The shed should have an outside

window and this should be wired over, yet still be able to be opened to allow ventilation.

Nesting materials should be provided for whatever cage or enclosure is decided on. I would suggest that this be of soft, sweet smelling meadow hay. As mentioned above, peat is the best floor covering as this absorbs urine and faeces better than wood shavings. Food should be

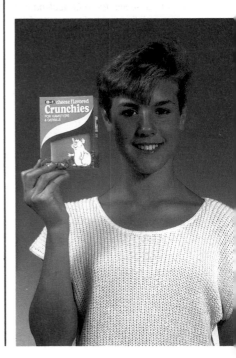

In addition to the standard meals, rodent treats of all varieties can and should be given as a supplement to the diet as well as a welcomed treat.

provided in strong heavy earthenware bowls that cannot be tipped over easily, while water should be provided in stainless steel tubed water bottles. I find that bowls are not a good idea for water as they can be upset too easily, thus causing a wet cage.

Cages, both indoor and outdoor, should be scrubbed at least four times a year with some form of disinfectant, then rinsed with clean water as many times as it takes to absorb the smell of the solution used. Nest boxes should be cleaned out periodically; this is particularly easy to do just after a litter has been weaned. Generally, chipmunks have no odor except for their urine and, as mentioned above, this is better absorbed by peat or bark chippings than by wood shavings.

Escapes

Should one of your chipmunks escape in the house, then they present few problems in returning them to their cage; however should this happen from an outdoor enclosure then you

Here we see a cross-section of a well-packed nest box loaded with hay, wood shavings, and several varieties of nuts. Such a box must be cleaned out occasionally and the stored food replaced with fresh food of the same type.

may have problems. If only one individual escapes, you may find that if left alone and given access to the aviary or cage then it will return to its own nest box before nightfall. However I should point out that should a pair escape then you are unlikely to have them return and, if they breed and establish a breeding group, in certain countries, for example, Great Britain, you would be liable to prosecution under the law as you will be deemed to have introduced an alien species to the countryside. Chipmunks are quite likely to survive in many countries if allowed to escape. The Siberian Chipmunk has already become established in certain areas of France, West Germany, the Netherlands and Austria, all as a result of escapes from pet homes. It is also reported that Siberian Chipmunks were introduced to the Prefecture of Tiba in Japan in the 1930's and that in 1906 a Mr. Sargood unsuccessfully tried to

This is a cut-away depiction of a wooden nest box originally made for birds which would serve well for chipmunks as well; it resembles a hollow tree.

release a pair of Eastern Chipmunks at Dunedin, New Zealand.

BUYING A CHIPMUNK

What age or sex or combination of chipmunks to buy really depends on what you ultimately require from them. I must say at this point that I have rarely found that single sex groups do well together although, as with many aspects of the care of chipmunks, this may well change as more and more individuals are bred in captivity.

If breeding is required obviously you will require a pair: one of each sex. This may sound a strange statement to make but please believe me that although you assume that a pair means one of each sex, others may not. It is always best to ask the seller to double check. It is best too, to try to obtain unrelated individuals unless you are attempting to breed for a particular colour or species and/or are unable to obtain unrelated stock. Breeding animals can be of any age up to about four years. At this age if they are not tame they are not likely to be easy to handle, but as breeding individuals this is

To an unexperienced eye it may be difficult to distinguish between a male and a female chipmunk. If you are at all in doubt, ask the dealer; even if you are not, it is a good idea to get a second opinion.

Health is probably the single most important consideration when purchasing a chip; the animal should be bright-eyed and alert, active, and feeding well.

not so important. Be wary of young animals labelled as breeding stock if they are under two years of age and have not bred. They may be potential breeders but no one can tell if a pair of young animals will settle down to breed.

If only a single individual is required for a pet then you will require an animal that is as young as possible, for example, 8-16 weeks. I have rarely found that animals over this age tame down completely.

When buying a chipmunk of any type or age, always choose one that is lively, with a good shine to its coat. It should have bright eyes and be without cuts and scars. Also, ensure that the tail is full. A damaged tail does a lot to destroy the charm of this species. It may be a sign of an imported or older animal. A damaged tail may be acceptable if the animal *is* of totally unrelated blood to introduce to your stud or a proven breed. But it may also be the sign of a trouble maker.

Animals that are over-aggressive to each other or to humans should be avoided. It is probably best to try to obtain individuals at the same time and if at all possible from the same place, although, if obtaining unrelated stock this is at times not possible. Buying at different times from

Although chipmunks are not odourous animals, a layer of cedar bedding will mask any odours which happen to occur.

One way to distinguish the sexes of rodents is to note the distance between the genital opening and the rectal opening; there is a greater distance between those of the male than there is between those of the female.

different places may mean that you will get animals that will not take to each other and you are then left with animals that you don't need or can't use. It is wise, therefore, to enter into an agreement with the seller of the animal that should it not fit in with your others you may return it, provided it is still in top condition. A pair that fight rarely settle down and make good breeding animals.

Many pet shops will be able to obtain stock for you as chipmunks are now much more readily available than even two years ago. However, should you require a coloured variety or a very young individual, then you are on the whole unlikely to be able to get such from a pet shop unless they breed their own stock. This is when private breeders come in; a source of this kind is useful in that they will be able to tell you the exact age and parentage of all the stock they have for sale.

Chipmunks should, in my mind, ideally be fed twice a day, once in the morning and once at night, or I should say more accurately, in the evening, as despite what many people think, chipmunks are not that nocturnal. They are up and about most of the day every day, unless the weather is very bad or it is winter.

As with most rodents, the basic diet is made up of various seeds and cereals with the addition of fruits, vegetables and, to a lesser extent, some form of protein. This latter is an area that is the cause of some debate with which I shall be dealing a little later. Firstly let us deal with the basics—seeds and cereals.

Most pet shops sell a basic rodents diet, although this is usually sold under the title "hamster mix." This is not fully suitable for your chipmunks, but it is a basis on which to build.

As you are probably aware, if food is obtained in bulk it will work out more cheaply in the long run, but if you have only a few animals, it can also go bad before you can use it and in the end cost more. You must therefore decide what amount is the most suitable for you to obtain at any one time. I usually purchase a large amount of ready mix diet and to this add items that individual species require. However, you may wish to obtain smaller bags of different items and mix these individually for each group of chipmunks or even for each individual animal.

Nibble sticks can be hung in the cage to provide your pet with a nutritious, teeth-grooming treat.

You will soon find that each chipmunk, like each human, has its likes and dislikes and it is a waste of time giving some types of food to some individuals. However, it is also important to remember that, like children, if allowed, they

However you decide to buy your foods, I would suggest that the following be included in all the basic mixtures; the proportions will again depend on your animals. The following are just guidelines that work for me and my animals; to this

A potpourri of flavour sits below this hungry critter. Feeding in this volume is of course not recommended for a single pet. It was done in this instance to determine this little one's favourite foods.

may well eat only their favourite foods and thus make themselves ill by not eating their correct diet. It is also true that certain foods will be eaten at one time of the year and totally ignored at others.

you can add or subtract as you gain experience.

Oats These often form the basis on which the diet is built. They may be purchased in different forms, the two major types being whole or crushed. I prefer the latter for although there appears to be a little more waste with this type, the husks of the whole oats are very sharp and can, when pouched by the chipmunks, harm the delicate lining of their pouches.

Wheat Along with oats this can be used as a basic food stuff; it is often used in equal parts with oats. Wheat is very rich in

The favourite time of the day for the chipmunk is feeding time; one will literally rise to the occasion in anticipation of that first tasty morsel.

In addition to proper feeding, proper exercise is essential for good health.

Vitamin E and is said to greatly assist fertility. I find that on the whole my animals are not keen on wheat and take it only in small amounts, wasting a lot of it.

Maize or Corn Again obtained in different forms, the most easily available is probably flaked. A useful item in the diet as there is little to no waste; it is a heating food and is thus very important in the winter and autumn. Too much in summer can however cause overheating and thus induce the animal to scratch and break the skin into open wounds.

Pelleted Foods Obtainable in a number of forms usually labelled for the animals for which they are suitable, i.e., rabbit, cavy, chinchilla, and rat. I would avoid those labelled for rabbits as they usually contain an antibiotic and on occasions this has caused problems for chipmunks as they are not designed for their system which is very different from that of a rabbit. I have found that the cavy or rat pellets are the most suitable. The rat pellet is usually much bigger than the cavy pellet and thus may not be suitable for young stock. Basically, pelleted foods are a compounded food and contain a balanced amount of food and vitamins (cavy pellets are usually high in vitamin C which I find very useful for chipmunks). They are a useful addition to the diet but should not be regarded as a suitable diet on their own.

Sunflower Seed Relished by chipmunks, being rich in Vitamin E and vegetable oils. They are a useful tidbit as well as a diet requirement. However, they are rather like sweets and will be overeaten if fed too often. They can cause an individual to become overweight and thus cause breeding problems.

Peanuts Another favourite item on the list for chipmunks; they tend to have the same advantages and disadvantages as sunflower seeds. Give only a few in the basic diet and then they will be relished even more when used as a tidbit.

Biscuits Many different forms of biscuits are sold for both dogs and cats and I have found that chipmunks will try a lot of different forms; one of mine particularly liked a fish variety of cat biscuit. They form a useful part of the diet by giving the animal something on which to

A chipmunk will voraciously eat most wild fruits and vegetables; extreme care must be taken, however, to avoid gathering any foods that have been sprayed with pesticides or other toxic chemicals.

One of the easiest ways to become the friend of a chipmunk is to hand-feed it one of its favourite treats.

chew that is very hard. Different sizes also help the animals with exercises for the paws and cheek pouches.

Nuts Chipmunks love nuts of all types. I shall not list them here as many have different names in different parts of the country. However all nuts are useful although some may well have too hard an outer shell for some chipmunks, particularly young animals, to chew through. This can be rectified by cracking a small hole in the outer shell.

Many items may be added to the above and variety is recommended in order to make the food interesting. Never feed exactly the same additions to the basic diet each day. Like yourself, chipmunks easily get bored by seeing the same old thing put in front of them day after day.

Vegetables Although many different vegetables are available in the shops, it is often quite useful to grow just a few of your own in the garden; then you will always have something fresh to give your pets.

Lettuce Although this is a most popular food for all types of pet rodents it is not really a good food particularly when fed in large amounts as it can cause a dangerous liver complaint. But don't misunderstand me. Lettuce is a useful food as it contains a lot of water (in fact something like 95%) as well as vitamins; it is only large amounts that should not be given.

Cabbage This too should not be fed in large amounts. The outer leaves are the most beneficial and it is usually just this area that the housewife discards. The so-called white cabbage is the lowest of all in food value.

Cauliflower Perhaps the most useful of all the "green" vegetables as it has a less drastic effect on the system of the individual. The leaves and stalk that are discarded are the best food value and the flowers or florets are also loved by both young and old stock.

Whether fresh green vegetables or pre-made pellet food, all foods should be given to your pet in clean, safe, heavy earthenware bowls.

Chicory A wonderful food that is now becoming more familar and therefore easier to obtain. It has a valuable amount of vitamins in it.

Kale An often overlooked vegetable that can be provided as a green food. All the plant can be used, so there is no waste.

Root vegetables These vary from season to season and it appears that certain

A water bottle, preferably with a metal spout, should be hung at an easily reached height.

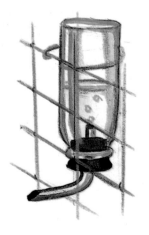

individuals will take a dislike to certain items; however, carrots are usually taken.

Fruit Various fruits will be accepted at different seasons when they are available in the shops. The following is a list of fruit that my own animals have eaten: sweet apple, oranges, grapes, avocado pear, blackberries, strawberries, peaches, plums (these last two should have the stones removed as it is thought that they may be toxic to chipmunks). You will undoubtedly find a lot more that you can add to this list.

Many other items may be added to the diet and these can include the following. Remember, however, that if you are collecting items from the wild or even your garden, be sure that they are washed well before feeding to the animals and that they haven't been sprayed with any chemicals. Chipmunks like a number of different flowers including marigolds, nasturtiums,

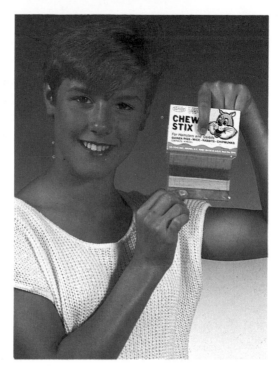

Chew Stix are one of the most enjoyable ways for your chipmunk to keep its front incisors in check.

roses, sweet peas, asters, and cornflowers. They also like many of the wild flowers such as clover, watercress, chickweed, dandelion, yarrow, and many others.

Now for the item that some people think is an important part of the diet and others think should be left out. In the wild, the chipmunk is known to raid birds' nests and eat both the eggs and the nestlings. I feel, therefore, that the diet of the chipmunk in captivity should reflect this and include in addition to the above, meat or eggs once or twice a week. I usually feed only small amounts of the following and never more than one item at a time: hard boiled or raw egg, tinned dog food, raw meat, meal worms, crickets and earthworms. I never feed very much and remove any uneaten food very quickly. Some individuals refuse to take these items while others will totally empty the food dish to search for them.

As with all animals, drinking water should be

The common grey squirrel is a distant relative of the chipmunk; it is a tree dweller, yet it has similar feeding habits. Indeed, there is much for the pet owner to learn from many of the chipmunk's relatives.

available at all times.

Lastly, please don't forget that, like the Grey Squirrel and the hamster, the chipmunk stores a great deal of its food. Therefore, please ensure that you do not overfeed items that are likely to go bad if stored. It is also important to remember that when you clean the cage, aviary or nest box, should you find a food store, always replace a little of the food either with some that is already there, if it is clean or with fresh food of similar nature.

Should a chipmunk find its food store regularly emptied it may retain food in its pouches all the time which will lead to problems.

Food and Water Pots

Food pots need to be very robust for chipmunks. Although stainless steel pots may be used, they are generally not very heavy and can easily be overturned by these animals. Glazed earthenware pots are much better; they are much heavier and yet just as easy to keep clean. Both the seed/cereal and the vegetable diet may be offered in such pots. Size of the pots will of course depend very much on the number of animals each cage or aviary contains.

The easiest and by far the best method of providing water is by means of a sealed water bottle with a spout, operating on the gravity flow system. Although a number of different types of spout are available, I find that the only ones really suitable for the chipmunk are those made of stainless steel. The position of the water bottle is important. You must ensure that it is within easy reach of the animal although to some extent the height is not too important as most chipmunks will climb the wire of the cage to reach the spout. Make sure that the water bottle fits firmly in place and that the animals' jumping about the cage and the use of the bottle will not dislodge it.

Naturally both water bottles and bowls should be cleaned regularly.

Chipmunks can become rather possessive of their food. If you don't want your pet to have something, don't give it to him, for taking it away may end in a heated dispute.

HANDLING AND SEXING

Unless obtained at a young age and well tamed, chipmunks do not like being handled and may bite extremely hard. This is not to say that chipmunks, even when acquired as adults, cannot be tamed. Far from it—many of them are very easy to handle but winning the confidence of a chipmunk enough to allow you to handle it is a much more difficult thing to do than with, say, a hamster. In fact, some people have likened taming a chipmunk to taming a Parrot.

Basically there are no hard and fast rules to taming an adult—it requires merely care, patience, and above all, *understanding*, especially of the fact that some individuals, however treated, will never allow themselves to be handled. The easiest way in which to tame an adult is in a large aviary type accommodation, one in which you can sit and allow the animals to come and smell, touch and climb on you, yet at the same time they are able to run away from you or keep you at a distance and thus feel "safe." By merely sitting and allowing the animals to come to you, you will find that gradually they will begin to climb over you and take tidbits from your hands. Eventually some will begin to push themselves up against your hand during this process, thus actually asking you to stroke them. Never rush the process, never attempt to pick the animal up unless it is able to jump away from you and therefore not feel trapped. To be blunt, one silly mistake and taking things too quickly can undo a month's long hard work.

Facing Page: A chip is most easily tamed in a large, walk-in type aviary. Here they feel safe and will often come to you on their own— sometimes rather surprisingly.

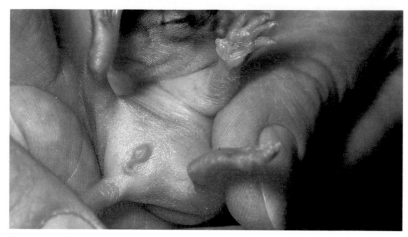

To an experienced eye, determining the sex of even a very young chip is not diffi-cult. Here we see an eight-day-old female.

As I said above, there are no hard and fast rules and there are therefore no real ways in which to tell you to proceed. What works with one individual will not necessarily work with another. One thing that can be firmly used as a rule to my mind, however, is that what a chipmunk hates above all else is to be grabbed; it is this that will cause an individual to bite.

If a chipmunk is obtained from a breeder, with time and care they will usually have gone to the trouble of hand-taming their young stock. To my mind hand-tamed stock are in some ways worth double the cost of untamed individuals. Hand-taming young homebred stock is a simple matter. Most females that are used to the presence of their owners will allow you to look into the nest box, even if they themselves are not hand-tame. Once it is clear that the litter is moving around and about to open their eyes, at about 12 days, begin to lift them gently out of the nest box and get them used to your scent and the feel of your hands on them. This does not have to be a very long session but should ideally take place every day. Once their eyes are open, keep this up and gradually you will find that they will be climbing all over you whenever you come within reach and even allow you to do exactly what their parents hate, clasp them around the belly.

It is possible to pick up some individuals by cupping or lifting by the scruff of the neck but it is difficult and I would not advise it, especially with strange or newly acquired animals.

Chipmunks are difficult to capture, even tame ones, especially in an outdoor enclosure. They are agile, to say the least, and a long continuous chase without a break is extremely stressful and should be avoided at all costs. This is particularly true with pregnant or nursing females. The best

way to capture them in this situation is with a soft butterfly net. This can be quickly and gently placed over the individual who is then gathered into the base

Chipmunks, like most small animals, are initially timid creatures. Don't overstress them; let them come to you. Never drag a chipmunk forcefully out of its nest box.

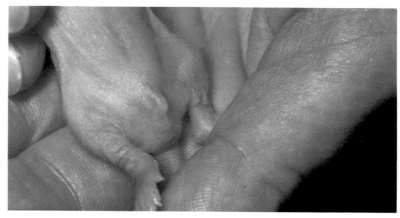

Pictured here is an eight-day-old male. Note the difference in the distance between its genital "bump" and its anal opening.

of the net and brought to your chest. Be careful at this stage as you are more likely to be bitten than at any other point. I would advise that you obtain a good pair of thick leather gloves for handling chipmunks.

Once you have netted your chipmunk, place your right hand firmly across its back and with the left hand supporting it underneath, lift it from the net. It can also be lifted with the right thumb and forefinger round the thick of the neck and supporting it underneath with the left hand.

To sex your chipmunk, gently turn it over on to its back with its genitals facing outward and the right hand holding it for support just below the forelimbs. Determine the sex by the distance between the anus and the genitals—the distance being greater in the male than in the female.

Lastly, two things to remember: *never* lift a chipmunk by the tail unless it is held very close to the base (very near the body) or it may shed and, unless very used to being handled, chipmunks bite first and ask questions after!!!

Siberian Chipmunks in captivity show an annual cycle similar to those in the wild. Births occur from late February through to late September or even early October. There are usually two peak periods of breeding, one in the early spring and one in midsummer. It is generally correct to say that those animals retained in the house are likely to begin breeding earlier and continue longer than those housed outside.

To some extent, breeding appears to be governed by both the climate and the day length. In fact it seems to be that extended day length, often used to increase breeding in other rodent species, actually prevents such increase in the chipmunk. Chipmunks generally do not breed in the autumn or winter, although, with the increasing breeding in captivity this may not always be the case.

Most Siberian Chipmunks breed only once a year, but some breed both in the spring and again when the first litter is weaned and removed from the cage of the parents.

Many begin breeding in the spring or summer of the year following their birth, i.e., at the age of eight to 14

The chase is on! Here a male is investigating the female's cage. If the female should demonstrate receptiveness to the male, then mating can begin.

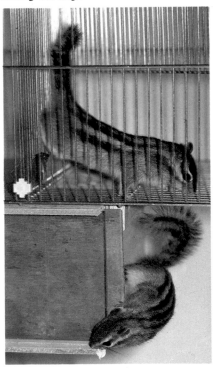

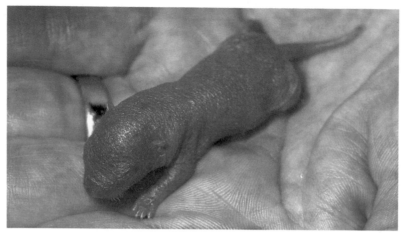

This delicate creature is a one-day-old chipmunk. Hand-rearing can begin at this early age. Utmost care must be taken; these less-than-one-inch living things are blind, extremely dependent, and extremely fragile.

months. The upper age limit for breeding appears actually to be governed by the death of the individual rather than any age limit.

The first signs of breeding conditions are usually that of the descending of the testes of the male into the scrotum early in January and the females starting to come into heat approximately two weeks later, in early February. In the wild this is probably to allow the male a period of time to establish a territory before the female is ready to mate.

The oestrus cycle, as the heat period of the female is called, lasts three days with an interval of about 14 days between each period. It appears that males are attracted to a female by scent, although the females do utter very frequent calls or "chips." This is usually from a very high point in their territory and more often than not on the second day of their cycle. At this time the female will usually allow the male to mate without any

becomes noticeably larger.

The actual mating is very difficult to describe in accurate detail as I have found that different pairs tend to perform in different

There are many ways to introduce a male to a female. If the male is well tamed, then as basic a procedure as shown here can be used—simply allow the male to walk around the outside of the female's cage until the female demonstrates receptiveness to him.

preliminary courtship. I have found it most easy to introduce strange animals together for breeding at this time. It is perhaps also interesting to note that when a female is in oestrus and the male has actual access to her, his scrotum

ways. For example, I have observed females standing perfectly still for the male with the tail lifted and held slightly to one side while others have barely stood still while the male mounted. Both resulted in litters. Mating does however usually take place after a short chase and each copulation is over quite quickly.

The gestation period usually lasts from 28 to 35 days, although this is only a guideline and some females may not conform to it. During this period the female will remain totally active, although she may remain in her nest box throughout the day of the actual birth and quite often the major part of the following day as well.

Litter size ranges from one to eight individuals in the wild but as many as 13

If you wish to house a male and a female in the same location, a single cage such as this one is useful. Allowing access through the wire mesh trap door system between the floors, the cage lets the male or female enter the other's territory unaided when you open the hatch.

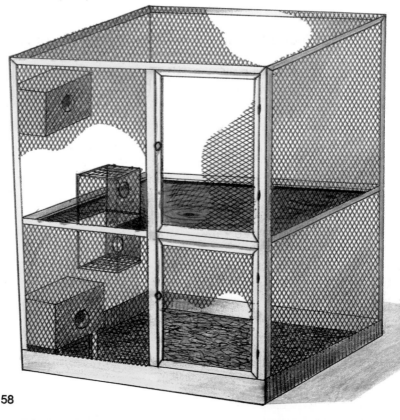

Here you see huddled in a nest a litter of eight-day-old chips.

has been recorded both in the wild and captivity. The usual litter in captivity appears to be four or five although, recently, I have received more and more reports of litters numbering eight.

The young are born naked and blind; their eyes open at about 14 days and during this first period the babies are extremely vocal, being clearly heard outside the nest boxes. They tend to begin to appear outside the nest box at about 35 days of age, but again this does vary from approximately 30-38 days. At this point they are in appearance very small adults. They still suckle from their mother at first but are usually weaned at about seven to ten days after emerging from the nest.

In the wild, a litter would appear to stay together for approximately six to eight weeks after leaving the nest. However, in captivity the early removal of the young, for example at six to seven weeks of age, may well encourage the production of a second litter.

I am often asked, "Is it safe to look at the litter in the nest?" This really depends on the calmness of the female and the situation of the nest box. Providing that the female is calm and doesn't panic whenever she sees you, you should be able to examine litters from about 48 hours of age, although with a first litter, I really feel that this is best left until the litter is about seven days old. At this age it is also easier to sex the youngsters. Naturally, the older the young are, the more active they will be and thus more difficult to catch and begin to hand-tame. Most females appear not to be all that worried by the examination of their young after the first week, although a few may well move them from one nest box to another once you have looked at them.

Not every pair of chipmunks will produce young. There are a number of stages in reproduction and all these various stages must be successful for a litter to be produced. Therefore if your pair or group appears to be getting on quite well yet fails to breed it is just as well to look and check if any of the following possible causes apply.

As mentioned above, climate and day length are both important, particularly if they are retained indoors or in a conservatory that is lighted at night. Cage size is important, especially to litter size; I know of much bigger litters from animals retained in large outdoor cages than those in indoor ones. Yet numbers of chipmunks per cage or cage size per chipmunk does not appear as important as does the cage itself, which should ideally be as wide as tall. It is important to provide at least one nest box per adult animal in each cage and if at all possible these should be at approximately the same height. It may not really be worth it but I usually try to provide at least one extra box for each pair of individuals. This

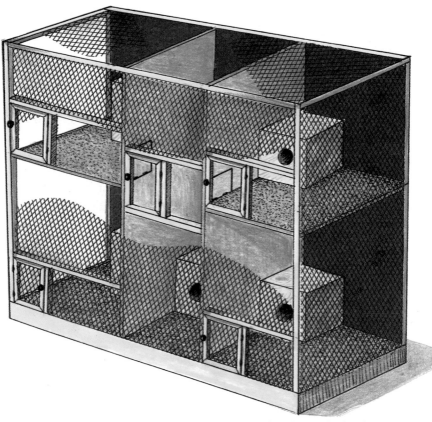

This is a sketch of a multiple breeding system in which males can be bred with two or more females with little intervention on the part of the owner.

suggests to me that space for activity as well as personal territory is important.

The presence of other rodent species appears to hinder reproduction; probably this has something to do with odours from the other species overpowering that of the chipmunk. Television transmissions can also be a factor in causing severe stress to chipmunks and in this condition females have been known to kill and eat their young.

Longevity

Chipmunks are relatively long-lived compared with many rodents of similar size. On the whole it appears that females live longer than males. From records produced by a number of people, few males appear to survive much over five years of age, the average being approximately 2½ years, whereas most females appear to live to approximately four years although nine, ten and even twelve years have been recorded for females.

Grouping

By far the most successful grouping of the Siberian Chipmunks in captivity for breeding is the pairing of two animals of the opposite sex. This may well sound a strange statement to make but a pair is not regarded by all as a male with a female. Many people, dealers included, regard a pair as two individual animals regardless of sex. However, even animals of the opposite sex cannot be guaranteed to breed. As stated elsewhere, it does not really matter what type of cage is provided so long as the cage meets the requirements of the individuals it contains. It is true to say that on the whole, successful breeding is achieved more often in an outside cage or aviary than in an indoor one.

If both individuals are new to you, and also to each other, they are quite likely to fight when introduced; therefore they are best introduced to a new cage at the same time. The uncertainty of their new surroundings often prevents fighting. This is more so for individuals of breeding age than those under 12 months of age. Should you purchase a breeding or established pair, introduction to a new cage usually presents no problems at all.

If you already possess one of a pair and then wish to introduce a new partner, I have found that the most successful way of doing this than when the female is introduced to the male. The exception to this may be on the second day of the female's cycle.

I have rarely found that colonies are totally

If the female is at the second day of her oestrus cycle, then there should be little trouble in getting the pair to mate.

is to allow the male the run of the cage or aviary for at least 24 hours before the introduction of the female. People have informed me that they have successfully introduced males to females' cages, but I have found that this is much more likely to result in fights successful, especially for more than a year, without major outside interference and the removal of individuals. It appears that quite large areas are required and at least two females should be present for each adult male in the colony. However, fighting appears to be much more common in chipmunks retained in this situation than in pairs. Here I am referring to colonies made up of adult or mature individuals, not those containing an adult pair plus their offspring of the year.

As stated in the chapter on caging, each individual should have a nest box. I would also suggest that there be at least one extra box for every three animals. A number of hollow logs or pipes on the floor of the cage are also useful to allow the submissive animals of the colony to escape the unwanted attentions of the dominant animals. Quite often in colonies only the most dominant females will breed and the numbers of the individuals per litter appear as low as those produced by pairs retained in a small cage situation. The other major problem with colonies is that exact parentage is difficult to know and it is far more difficult to tame individuals.

Occasionally, a female will for some reason or another—perhaps due to the death of her original male—refuse to accept a new mate. Often at this stage this female has to be left out of a breeding programme or given away as a non-breeding individual. This can be a great blow to a breeding programme, particularly if she is an unusual colour or type. However, this does not always have to be the case. For example a female that has lost her mate but still has her litter or is pregnant will often accept one of her sons as her consort the following spring. This may be achieved by not removing the chosen male with the rest of the litter at weaning or on the sale of the rest. However care should be taken to monitor her continued acceptance of the male.

Some females will not accept any male on a permanent basis. Should this be your situation it may be possible to "hand mate"

This baby is 15-days old. Note the definitive markings on the back. Note also the development of the claws.

her. This means allowing her access to a male only when she is in heat and remove him after mating. This is difficult to achieve and to my mind should really be used only as a last resort. Again, the female should be introduced to the cage of the male. Introduce her on the second day of her cycle, the day when she is calling and basically demanding a male to mate with. There may be a slight play fight on meeting but by this time you should be able to tell a serious fight from a mock battle. Don't forget, never attempt to stop a fight with bare hands. Should a serious fight occur, remove the female and try her again later the same day or the next day. As soon as the male has mounted and copulation begun, you may leave them alone for a while. Never allow a female, if she is known to attack the male, to remain in his cage for longer than a few hours,

Copulation is quick and courtship generally brief if the female is ready to receive the male.

and never overnight.

Another way of achieving this is to place the female in a smaller cage within that of the male's. When the female appears ready to allow the male to mount her, he having access to her odour, etc., through the bars of the cage but she is not able to actually bite him, release her and allow them to mate. This is also a useful way to introduce a new female to any overaggressive male.

Single individuals and single sexed pairs and groups appear to work quite well and be happy when breeding is not required. However, remember that adult individuals of the same sex, previously used for breeding, are unlikely to tolerate each other.

Finally, don't forget that a male removed from the female and her young may be difficult to reintroduce to the female. Allow him to stay. He will rarely harm the young at all and, in fact, some males, unlike those in the wild, will actually help with the rearing.

CHIPMUNK GENETICS

As explained earlier, the Siberian Chipmunk occurs in the wild in a wide variety of colour variations. All these have one thing in common: they are all basically a reddish/brownish/greyish colour commonly called Agouti. These colour variations cannot appear to be bred for; in other words, by mating two reddish animals together, there is no certainty that reddish babies will be obtained even in later generations. The only exception to this appears to be the so-called Cinnamon. This variety has occurred quite often recently and I believe may be descended from stock imported into this country in the late 1960's, early 1970's, from the Japanese Island of Hokkaido. These individuals were slightly finer-boned than those of the mainland subspecies

Although in the wild there are several colour varieties of the Siberian Chipmunk, many of these seem not to be bred with much predictability in captivity. Perhaps with the increased populations of captive chipmunks and more focused efforts by serious breeders, this will change in the future.

and were also more noticeably reddish/cinnamon. Unfortunately, stock of this island subspecies were not retained in separate populations from the mainland form, most of which originated from Korea, and thus the majority of animals in the UK carry blood from both groups. However, in recent years individuals have been noticed in litters born in the UK that are finer-boned and more reddish/cinnamon in colouration. I feel that these may be a throwback to the Hokkaido stock. This may mean that there is a separate gene known as a recessive.

One true mutation does occur and this is indeed a recessive mutation. This is the dilute white or White Chipmunk. It is not, however, an albino; it is a pale cream to white, with pale beige stripes and tail, and has dark reddish ruby eyes. A true albino would have no stripes and have pink eyes. The dilutes are born the same colour as their normal litter mates but after a few days when the normal babies begin to turn to a dark brown the dilutes remain pinkish. Gradually they turn white and at this stage many people mistake them for albinos; however, in a few days faint brownish stripes begin to appear and at the time they leave the nest they appear as a sort of ghostly form of the normal.

It is highly likely that as chipmunks are more widely kept and bred more mutations will occur. If this should happen, it is important to know a little about genetics, particularly the difference between what is called a recessive and a dominant gene.

There are two forms of inheritance, recessive and dominant. The recessive is undoubtedly the most common form. A colour mutation is known to be recessive when it disappears in crosses with the original wild colour. For example, when the dilute

The Agouti colouration displayed by this baby chip is a dominant trait and is the most common of both wild-born and home-bred chipmunks. Eyedropper feeding is essential in the early weeks of hand-rearing.

white is mated to a normal, unrelated individual, all the offspring will be of the wild or Agouti colour. This not only proves that the dilute is recessive to the Agouti but also that the Agouti is dominant to the dilute.

So if a Dilute is mated to an Agouti, you will obtain 100% normal or Agouti coloured babies. If mated together, however, these young will themselves give birth to 75% normal young and 25% Dilute. If you mate one of the babies back to one of the dilute parents, they will give birth to 50% normal and 50% dilute young.

This shows what is known as the typical 3:1 ratio, which plays an important part in the genetics of any animal. The fact that the dilute colour does not reappear until the second generation need not worry you because once it has recurred, the dilute are true breeding and will not revert to the normal colour if mated together.

The first cross of any two colours is known as the F1 generation and when these are mated together, they produce the F2 generation.

A dominant form of inheritance does not occur in the chipmunk at present. A dominant colour does not disappear in crosses with the normal colour.

One point to remember is that whether you are dealing with a dominant or a recessive inheritance, a colour is not necessarily lost if it does not appear in the young. An animal which is the wild normal colour may be "split." This means that it carries in its genes another colour and when this animal is mated to another carrying the same colour, another "split" individual, they will produce young actually showing this colour. Thus two "normals" can produce a dilute animal.

Breeding Records

When breeding chipmunks or for that matter any other species to any extent, records should be maintained to avoid breeding related animals together too often.

The importance of keeping accurate and up-to-date records is particularly essential when breeding for colour mutations such as the Dilute White. It is also important that a breeder can see at a glance which stock has been bred from which individual and which pair has produced the best results.

By far the simplest way of doing this is to give each individual animal a card. This may be attached to the cage or stored in an index box or even recorded in a home computer. On each card record such information as the name of the animal, its parents, grandparents, colour, date of birth, the date of all litters borne or sired by it, the size of each litter and the

This is not an Albino Chipmunk, it is a genuine mutation (a ruby-eyed white chipmunk) owned by Mrs. Christine Wright of Latchingdon Nr Chelmsford, Essex.

individuals bred.

From the information contained on these cards, detailed pedigrees can be formulated and should a rare mutation be produced, its ancestry can be traced back and it may then be possible to reproduce others by the same means.

Pure Albino Chipmunk

Yet another genotype is appearing in the Siberian Chipmunk, a *pure* albino. Individuals of this type are pure snowy white, with bright pink eyes and no markings; they appear to be smaller and less robust than both the normal variations and the dilute white animals.

HAND-REARING BABY CHIPMUNKS

As far as I am aware, only Siberian Chipmunks have successfully been hand-reared from birth in the UK, but now that American species are becoming available this may soon change. I would like to think that as the different species develop in such a similar way that their rearing by hand would not be that different. At present there is no special preparation available to the general public for the hand-rearing of small rodents, so to some extent all hand-rearing is sadly trial and error. All I can say is that from talking to a number of people who have successfully hand-reared Chipmunks over the past few years the following appears to work; I am not saying that this is the only way to hand-rear, merely that this method has worked for others. The most important factor to remember in successful hand-rearing is the need to feed the individual(s) regularly. Animals as small as Chipmunks (a newborn being only about 3-4 cms in length) take such tiny amounts of food at any single feeding that it is extremely important to maintain the intake of nourishment. However, it is also very important to avoid feeding foods that are too rich. The first sign of an over-rich diet is diarrhea; unfortunately, unless the problem is quickly rectified death will be the outcome.

Hand-rearing can be a time-consuming and very tiring business, and this must be remembered before any attempt is made. Until the baby Chipmunk is three weeks old it will require feeding EVERY THREE HOURS DAY AND NIGHT. At four weeks you may drop the early or middle of the night feed job (i.e., between midnight and 6 a.m.). Should the baby be the runt of the litter you may need to increase the number of feedings from every three hours to every two until four weeks of age. To feed, use a dropper; you can often obtain those

Hand-rearing baby rodents—whether they're chipmunks or one of the closely related rodent species like the young ground squirrel shown here—requires considerable hard work and dedication, but the rewards make it all worth the while. In no other way can one achieve as loving and affectionate a chipmunk but through hand-rearing. Hand-rearing is for pet owners the truest way to achieve the ultimate bond between themselves and their pets.

marketed for very small kittens, and you will require the smallest available. When feeding you must do so very slowly and watch carefully all the while for bubbles at the nostrils or the sounds of choking, which indicate that the food is not entering the stomach but the lungs instead. Should this happen hold the baby gently by the hind legs until the lungs are again clear. Between feedings, the animal(s) should be kept in a box, in a nest made of soft tissue paper or cloth and lightly covered so as to allow air to get to the baby. The box must, naturally, be kept in a warm place, but not a hot place.

Don't forget to lightly stroke the baby's stomach after each feeding. Stroke towards the tail with a damp, warm piece of cotton wool to stimulate the bowels.

Hand-rearing Baby Chipmunks

Suitable Diet

From day 1-7: 1 part of evaporated milk to 2 parts water, with a pinch of glucose powder.

From day 8-30: 4 teaspoons of baby cereal; 1 teaspoon evaporated milk; ½ teaspoon of honey or glucose powder. This should be mixed together to the consistency of gruel.

Alternatively a prepared milk rearing food sold for kittens may be used.

When hand-rearing it may be useful to know what stage of development should be reached at what time. The following may be of help in this:

Day 10-12: Stripes show on the skin.

Day 12-14: Fur begins to appear through the skin.

Day 16: Looks like a miniature adult but still with the eyes closed.

Day 26-30: Eyes and ears open.

Day 30-35: Solid food taken.

To ensure the life and health of your baby chips, follow a sound diet plan and feed on the strictest schedule.

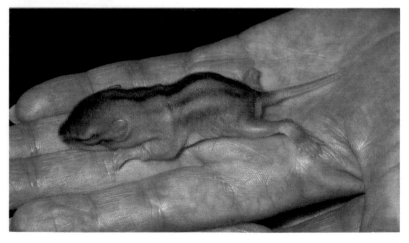

Most chipmunks are healthy throughout their lives, never have a day's illness and die of old age. But with increased inbreeding they are likely to develop slight problems. Bad management however, does account for a number of deaths. The majority of these are caused by bad feeding; in some cases the bad siting of cages and aviaries.

I am not saying that chipmunks are never ill. Therefore I shall mention a few of the more common ailments that may occur. Should your chipmunk appear ill and you are unsure what to do, please do not have a wild guess and try to treat it yourself; take the animal straight to your local veterinary surgeon.

Wounds and cuts As with most rodents, a chipmunk's flesh heals very quickly, and slight cuts and wounds are not in themselves dangerous at all. The most common cause of these

wounds are sharp edges to the climbing and bedding materials, edges to the cage and slight fights. Serious wounds do occur when strange individuals are introduced to each other and at these times great care should be taken. Only

A well-constructed cage, free of sharp objects and located in a draft-free or weather-proofed place, is one of the ways to ensure sound health.

very deep wounds or cuts need to be dealt with by the vet. Most cuts can be bathed in a mild antiseptic solution once a day. This may warrant removing individual animals from an outdoor enclosure or group

Excessive feeding of any one kind of food will lead to a dietary imbalance and possibly other complications. Feed wisely, feed in variety.

unless your animals are very tame and come to you. If your animal is not used to being handled, then it may well be worth not treating a very mild wound; just keep a very close eye on it for infections and allow nature to heal the wound itself.

Constipation A blockage of the intestines causes constipation. In the majority of cases this is caused by unsuitable bedding such as cotton wool, wood wastes, kapok, or newspaper. All bedding should be replaced with good soft meadow hay and fresh foods should be given in larger amounts than usual. Should the constipation persist for more than 24 hours, consult your vet.

Diarrhoea The opposite of constipation. The most common cause is the over-feeding of fresh vegetables or a sudden change in diet. Females that are nursing do tend to produce a little looser feces than normal and this is nothing to worry about.

Overgrown teeth On rare occasions, the teeth of Chipmunks become overgrown due to the over-feeding of too much soft food. At these times the individual should be taken to your vet for the teeth to be trimmed and the animal's diet should be changed to include a much higher proportion of nuts and biscuits on which the teeth may be worn down. Even rarer is the case of misaligned teeth. This often occurs in both adults and young when the teeth or jaws have been damaged by an accident or in a fight. In many of these cases the clipping of the teeth will have to be performed at least once a month and this can cause a great deal of stress to individuals. Should this be the case, it may be kinder to ask your vet to put the individual to sleep.

Hibernation This is not really an ailment or illness but it seems appropriate to

A cardboard tube can serve as a play-tunnel for your pets and can also be used as a chewing object which will help to wear down the teeth and provide extra bedding and nesting material. It will be enjoyed by your chipmunks just as it is by the gerbils shown below.

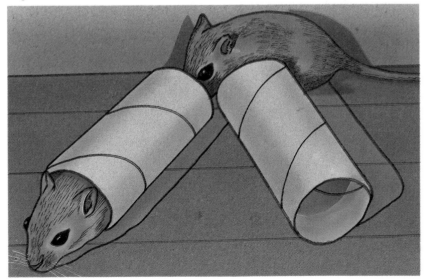

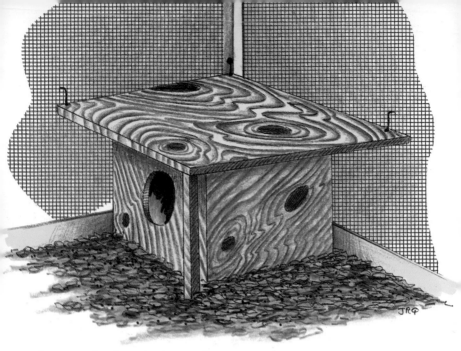

A warm and well-constructed nest box is essential for safe winter housing.

include it here. Chipmunks that are retained in outdoor enclosures all year around without access to heated accommodation often hibernate. This is usually in their nest box or if they have a peat or soil-based cage they may dig burrows. Hibernation does not appear to be harmful to Chipmunks and, indeed, in many areas of the wild they hibernate quite naturally. Two things should be borne in mind. One, they should be allowed to make a nest in which to hibernate that is in a good frost-proof position. Two, the animal should have been given a very good diet during the previous few months, in order that it be allowed to have a good fat supply on which to live while in hibernation.

For this reason I personally would not allow newly acquired animals to hibernate—just in case. Chipmunks do not, in fact, hibernate all winter but rather for odd days at a time when the weather is particularly bad.

CHIPMUNK SPECIES

The various *Eutamias* species and their distribution in the wild:

Eutamias sibiricus—Siberia, Mongolia; northern and central China; Korea and Hokkaido (Japan).

Eutamias alpinus—Sierra Nevadas (East central California).

Eutamias minimus—Yukon to Ontario and Wisconsin.

Eutamias amoenus— Southwestern Canada and Northwestern USA.

Eutamias townsendii— Extreme southwestern British Columbia to western Oregon.

Eutamias ochrogenys— Northwestern coast of California.

Eutamias senex—Central Oregon; northern California.

Eutamias siskiyou— Southwestern Oregon; extreme NW California.

Eutamias sonanae— Northwestern California.

Eutamias merriami— Central and southern California; Baja California.

Eutamias obscurus— Southern California; Baja California.

Eutamias dorsalis— Southwestern USA; northern Mexico.

Eutamias quadririttatus— Eastern Utah, Colorado, NE Arizona, New Mexico, extreme western Oklahoma.

There are many species of chipmunks; yet, there is generally little difference between each group.

RQ

Eutamias ruficaudus—
Southern British
Columbia; extreme
southwestern Alberta,
northeastern Washington,
northern and NW
Montana.
Eutamias canpies—South
central New Mexico;
extreme western Texas;
probably northern
Mexico.
Eutamias cinereicollis—
East central Arizona, SW
Mexico.
*Eutamias
quadrimaculatus*—East
central California.
Eutamias speciosus—
Mountains of eastern and
southern California.
Eutamias panamintinius—
SW Nevada and adjacent
parts of California.
Eutamias umbrinus—West
central USA.
Eutamias palmeri—
Southern Nevada.
Eutamias bulleri—West
central Mexico.

**Brief Description of the
Various** *Eutamias* **Species**
of Northern America

The head-and body-
length of the various
Eutamias species vary quite
widely from 80 to 160 mm
with the additional tail
length from 60 to 140 mm.
Coat colours and sizes vary
and I shall deal with each
species separately;
however, all have the
conspicuous and
characteristic five black or
blackish brown longitudinal
back stripes separated by
four whitish or buff stripes.
They vary greatly in both
habits and habitats from
species to species, but in
general they are more agile
and sprightly than the
eastern Chipmunks and are
more arboreal, less shy and
more social. Many inhabit
overlapping ranges from
lowland to mountaintop,
with the palest chipmunks
originating in the driest
areas and the darkest in the
most humid.

*Facing Page: A favourite pastime
with hobbyists and their chipmunks is
a sort of hide-n-find game of treats.*

Caught with its whole self in the cookie bag! If hungry and there is food, a chipmunk will find it.

Alpine Chipmunk, *Eutamias alpinus* A small species, generally a yellowish-grey with dark side stripes usually reddish or brownish, not blackish. A dark stripe down the middle of the back is usually black. The tail is bright orange below with a length of approximately 166-203 mm. This species inhabits the Sierra Nevada Mountains of eastern central California, from the timber line to 8,000' elevation. This is an area of sub-alpine forest.

Least Chipmunk, *Eutamias minimus* As the scientific name implies, this is one of the smallest of the Chipmunks, only 167-225 mm; it has however a very wide range and thus variable colouring. In drier regions, muted yellowish-grey above with tan dark stripes; in the moister areas, brownish grey with black side stripes; stripes continue to the base of the tail. Sides, orangish brown, belly greyish white. The tail is long, light brown above, yellowish below with hairs tipped black. Ears are noticeably tawny in front. It is the lightest in colour of all the Western Chipmunks. The range is wide and includes most of southern Canada from Ontario to south Yukon, from North Dakota down to New Mexico and west to NW California and SE Washington. In this wide area it inhabits sage brush desert, pastures, pine woods, cliffs and open coniferous forests.

Yellow Pine Chipmunk,
Eutamias amoenus One of the larger species, 181-245 mm. Brightly coloured ranging from tawny to pinkish-cinnamon, with very distinct stripes; Light stripes being whitish while the dark stripes are usually black. Sides and undersides of the tail brownish yellow. The top of the head is brown, ears are blackish in front and whitish behind. The range is from British Columbia south to northern California, east to west

Montana and northwest Wyoming, in the coniferous yellow pine forests.

Townsend's Chipmunk,
Eutamias townsendii
Another of the large species 221-317 mm. Dark brown in colour, often with rather wide, diffuse or at least indistinct blackish and light stripes on the head and continuing down the body. Lighter in summer than in winter. The back of the ears are noticeably bi-coloured; dusky on the front half, grey on back. The tail is long and bushy; blackish above with many white tipped hairs, bright reddish-brown below bordered with black and finely edged with white tipped hairs. The range is from extreme southern British Columbia south through most of west Oregon; in the humid coniferous and hardwood forests.

Similar species that at one time were regarded as subspecies of Townsend's but are now regarded as species in their own right by some authorities are: Allen's Chipmunk, *Eutamias senex,* of NE California and WC Oregon. Siskiyou Chipmunk, *Eutamias siskiyou,* of NE California and S Oregon. Yellow Cheeked Chipmunk, *Eutamias ochrogenys,* of NW California and SW Oregon.

Sonoma Chipmunk,

Eutamias sonomae A large noticeably brownish Chipmunk of from 220-227 mm in length, all the stripes on the back are indistinct, all about the same width; lighter stripes yellowish. Tail reddish below, but becoming paler towards the base, edged with buff. On the head, the dark stripes are reddish, with black spots behind the eyes and below the ears. The backs of the ears nearly uniform brownish in colour. They inhabit brushy open ground in redwood or yellow pine forests of Northwestern California.

Merriam 's Chipmunk,

Eutamias merriami A greyish brown species measuring between 208-280 mm. It has a distinct white belly, the stripes are nearly equal in width; indistinct, the dark stripes either grey or brown; only rarely black. Lighter stripes greyish. The tail is long, edged with buff or white. The range is limited to the brushlands, forested foothills and coniferous forests of southern California.

Cliff Chipmunk, *Eutamias dorsalis* A medium Chipmunk 195-277 mm. Greyish with the stripes on the body either indistinct or totally absent, yet often quite distinct on the sides of the head. Bushy tail rust red below. This species inhabits

Facing Page: Fruit or fungi? This chipmunk will dine first on a grape and maybe later on the mushroom cap.

the rocky areas, cliffs and juniper zones of Eastern Nevada, Utah, and extreme NW Colorado, Arizona and Western New Mexico.

Red Tailed Chipmunk,

Eutamias ruficaudus A large little-known brightly coloured Chipmunk. In colour it is a deep tawny above and on the sides; the rump, however, is grey contrasting greatly with the front part of the body. The tail is rufous above, dark reddish below. There are three median stripes on the back, black in colour, although the outer stripes are often brownish. The cheeks have two white and three brown stripes. It is found in the coniferous fir forests of SE British Columbia, NE Washington, N Idaho and Western Montana.

Grey Collared Chipmunk,

Eutamias cinereicollis This chipmunk reaches between 208-250 mm. Greyish in colour with a paler grey neck and shoulders. The

back stripes are black; side stripes pale grey and dark brown. It inhabits the coniferous forests of eastern central Arizona and SW New Mexico.

Long Eared Chipmunk,

Eutamias quadrimaculatus A fairly large, impressive, brightly coloured chipmunk with indistinct body stripes. The tail is reddish brown below edged with white. The ears are long with large white patch behind and dark, almost black, stripe below. It is a Chipmunk with a restricted range, being confined to the pine and fir forests of the Sierra Nevada Mountains at elevations of 3,600-7,300' in Eastern central California.

Lodgepole Chipmunk,

Eutamias speciosus A Chipmunk with a maximum size of 197-241 mm. Bright brown above with distinct stripes, these being medium to dark back stripes, but the outer ones are generally paler or often missing altogether. Outer light stripe bright white and broader than inner light stripes. The top of the head is brown. Black spots are present both in front and behind the eyes; stripes on the front of the head are often missing;

brightly coloured species, 192-220 mm. In colour it is reddish or tawny on the back; head and rump grey. Outer dark stripes on the back indistinct; inner ones reddish or even greyish.

Chipmunk chasing is a part of courtship behavior.

ears blackish in front, white behind. The tail has a black band about 1 inch wide on the underside near the tip.

The Lodgepole Chipmunk is restricted to eastern central California usually in the lodgepole pine and red fir stands.

Panamint Chipmunk,
Eutamias panamintinus A

The head is grey on top, with upper eye stripe black, lower one brown. The ears are tawny in front.

The habitat is the pinon-juniper forest in rocky areas of SW Nevada and southern central California.

Unita Chipmunk, *Eutamias umbrinus* Ranging from 196-243 mm. It is greyish above including the crown of the head, with wide, dark brown side stripes; white below; tawny wash on the sides. The tail is black tipped, white bordered with a tawny underside. The ears blackish in front, whitish behind. It inhabits a wide range of coniferous forest, mixed woods, etc., from Wyoming, Nevada, Western California, Utah, North Central Arizona, North Central Colorado.

Closely related and very similar species include the Colorado Chipmunk *Eutamias quadrivittatus,* from SE Utah, W Colorado, Northern New Mexico and northeast Arizona and Palmer's Chipmunk, *Eutamias palmeri,* from southern Nevada.

Habits of the American Western Chipmunks

As with the Siberian Chipmunk, in order to understand your chipmunk's requirements in captivity, it is worth taking a look at the Western American Chipmunk's behaviour in the wild.

The Western American Chipmunks vary considerably in both habits and habitats, but in general they are more agile and active than both the Eastern American and the Siberian; however they are on the whole very similar to the closely related Siberian.

As previously stated, the Western Chipmunks inhabit a very wide range of habitats, from the arid scrublands to the great stands of coniferous and deciduous forests.

As with the Siberian, the Western species dig their burrows in the ground or in old rotting logs, but unfortunately despite their wide range and in some areas close study above the ground, little is actually known about the detailed construction of their burrows. Generally, a tunnel appears to be about 60-90 cms in length terminating in a chamber about 30 cms below the surface. This small chamber contains a

The happy face of a well-fed (and still feeding) chipmunk.

nest as well as a store of seeds for winter food. Occasionally, some species inhabit holes in trees quite high up, but this is thought to be quite rare and usually due to ground conditions such as frequent floods.

It appears that total hibernation only occurs in areas where deep snow lies on the ground all winter thus preventing foraging for food.

There is generally only a single litter each year; second litters seem to be much rarer than in the Siberian.

Vocal calls appear to be about the same with all the species and very similar to the Siberian.

As with the Siberian, the

Westerns are quite social both in the wild and in captivity, although the Western American Chipmunks are not widely retained. Home ranges appear to overlap quite broadly and several individuals are often seen foraging close together in the same locations. These ranges appear to vary from less than an acre to several acres, usually depending on the quality of the habitat, the ranges of males always being larger than those of the females.

Diet includes nuts, fruit, grains, and vegetable matter of various kinds. For example wild berries, seeds of conifers and, in some areas, cactus fruits. In some areas, insects and small mammals are also taken.

The Eastern American Chipmunk, *Tamias striatus* A single species that in the wild inhabits the eastern United States and the southeastern areas of Canada.

Facing Page: Acrobatically inclined.

It is larger than the other species of Chipmunks with a head and body length of 137-186 mm and a tail length of 78-113 mm.

The background colour is reddish brown to chestnut and there are five black stripes, separated by pale stripes; the stripes fade into the reddish flanks and rump. The underparts are white to buffy and the feet are tan. The prominent short ears are edged with russet. The tail is reddish brown, well furred and yet not bushy. Overall the fur is straight, soft and quite fine.

On the whole, the Eastern Chipmunk is a rather solitary species and can be highly aggressive towards others of its own kind even in the wild. For this reason it is rarely retained in captivity. In the wild each adult defends a small home range. This range is based around and centred on the burrow, from which all intruders are chased away.

During the breeding season males congregate

Here a female chipmunk is exploring a new territory.

on the home range of an in-season female and compete for mating privileges. There are certainly no lasting pair bonds. For this reason Eastern Chipmunks should only be retained together during the short period in which the female is receptive to the male. Personally, I would suggest that a male should be introduced to the female cage only when she is actually calling loudly and showing obvious signs that she is ready to mate and that they be watched very carefully and parted as soon as fighting occurs. Should you not do this, you may well end up with one very dead male. This species has been retained in pairs in captivity but they are usually housed in very large enclosures with a great deal of cover and climbing areas.

Most Eastern Chipmunks become sexually mature in the spring of the year after they are born, although on rare occasions some females born in the very early spring may breed later the same year—usually very late summer or early autumn.

With a controlled climate, a readily available food supply, and an absence of predators, chipmunks in captivity can live to a ripe old age.

Generally the life span of this species is 2½-3 years, but in captivity, it may well attain a much greater age, even reaching 9 or 10 years. Mating in captivity generally reflects the habits in the wild, occurring during late March and early April. The gestation is about 31 days, usually only a single litter is produced each year,

A chipmunk checking its nesting box.

but some females will raise a second in captivity where food is easier to come by than in the wild. Litters number two to seven but average out at four. As with the Siberian they are naked and blind at birth and weigh approximately 3 grams.

They first venture out of the nest at about five weeks of age and are usually chased from the territory of the female by about six and a half to seven weeks. In captivity litters should be removed from the adult female's cage at this age or she may well begin to kill them. Although the litter may be retained together for a short period of time, eventually it will undoubtedly be necessary to cage the individuals separately.

It is, as a species, much more of a ground dweller than others and doesn't require quite such a tall cage or enclosure as the Western species and the Siberian. Likewise, the nest boxes need to be placed at a slightly lower level. They are very active throughout the day but rarely so at night.

Index

CHIPMUNKS
KW-181